SRA Open Court Reading

Comprehension and Language Arts Skills

Level 1

A Division of The McGraw-Hill Companies

Columbus, Ohio

www.sra4kids.com

SRA/McGraw-Hill

A Division of The McGraw·Hill Companies

2005 Imprint

Send all inquiries to:
SRA/McGraw-Hill
8787 Orion Place
Columbus, OH 43240-4027

Printed in the United States of America.

ISBN 0-07-569516-2

16 17 18 19   POH   09 08 07 06

Table of Contents

Name _____ Date _____

Capital Letters

Rule	Example
▶ People's names start with capital letters. The word *I* is always written with a capital letter.	▶ Tim Sandy Miller I

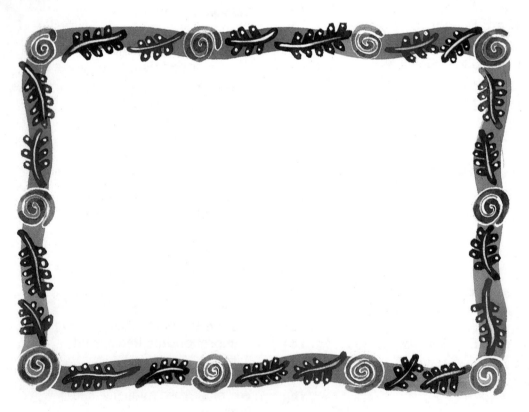

_____

‒ ‒

_____

Directions: Draw a picture of yourself. Write your name under the picture. Start it with a capital letter.

UNIT I   Let's Read! • **Lesson I** *Unit Introduction*

▶ Capital Letters

Practice

Directions: Draw a picture of two people in your family. Write their names under their pictures. Start each name with a capital letter.

MECHANICS

_____   _____

_ _ _ _ _ _ _ _ _ _ _ _ _ _ _ _ _   _ _ _ _ _ _ _ _ _ _ _ _ _ _ _ _ _

_____   _____

Writing Words

Rule	Example
▶ Letters make words.	▶ cat
	dog

Try It!

_____

- - - - - - - - - - - - - - - - - -

_____

_____

- - - - - - - - - - - - - - - - - -

_____

_____

- - - - - - - - - - - - - - - - - -

_____

Directions: Write as many words as you can.

UNIT 1   Let's Read! • **Lesson 2** *The Purple Cow*

Writing Words

Practice

1.

_____
- - - - - - - - - - - - - - -
_____

2.

_____
- - - - - - - - - - - - - - -
_____

3.

_____
- - - - - - - - - - - - - - -
_____

4.

_____
- - - - - - - - - - - - - - -
_____

5.

_____
- - - - - - - - - - - - - - -
_____

WRITER'S CRAFT

Name _____ Date _____

Capital Letters: Cities and States

Rule	**Example**
▶ Names of cities and states start with capital letters.	▶ New York Ohio Akron Florida Texas Tampa

Try It!

1. _____rizona_____

2. _____labama_____

3. _____rkansas_____

4. _____laska_____

UNIT 1 Let's Read! • **Lesson 6** *There Was Once a Fish*

▶ **Capital Letters**

Practice

Directions: Draw a picture of your city. Write the name of your city. Write the name of your state. Use capital letters.

MECHANICS

_____

- -

_____

_____

- -

_____

Order Words

Directions: Put the pictures in time order. Label them first, next, then, and last.

Rule	**Example**
▶ Some words organize writing.	▶ first next then last

_____

- - - - - - - - - - - - - -

_____

- - - - - - - - - - - - - -

_____

- - - - - - - - - - - - - -

_____

- - - - - - - - - - - - - -

▶ **Order Words**

Practice

Directions: Put the pictures in time order. Label them first, next, then, and last.

_____

- - - - - - - - - - - - - - - - - -

_____

_____

- - - - - - - - - - - - - - - - - -

_____

_____

- - - - - - - - - - - - - - - - - -

_____

_____

- - - - - - - - - - - - - - - - - -

_____

WRITER'S CRAFT

Sentences

Directions: Put a capital letter at the beginning of each sentence. Put a period at the end of each sentence.

Rule
▶ Sentences start with capital letters. Many sentences end with periods.

Example
▶ Frogs leap.

Try It!

1. irds fly

2. ogs run

3. ish swim

4. e have fun

▶ **Sentences**

Practice

Directions: Put a capital letter at the beginning of each sentence. Put a period at the end of each sentence.

5. ___ urtles crawl

6. ___ ats walk

7. ___ abbits hop

8. ___ e talk

MECHANICS

▶ Sentences

Directions: Write sentences using the words in the lists. Put a capital letter at the beginning of each sentence. Put a period at the end of each sentence.

Rule	**Example**
▶ Sentences tell a thought.	▶ Mice squeak.

birds   buzz

bees   sing

cows   bark

dogs   moo

1. _____

2. _____

3. _____

4. _____

UNIT I   Let's Read! • **Lesson 12** *The Chase*

Practice

fish	run
mice	swim
deer	fly
birds	jump

5. _____

6. _____

7. _____

8. _____

WRITER'S CRAFT

Comparing and Contrasting

Directions: Review "Mrs. Goose's Baby." Discuss each picture and have the children circle A if the picture shows how the goose and chick are alike and D if the picture shows how they are different.

A   D

A   D

A   D

A   D

A   D

A   D

UNIT 1   Let's Read! • **Lesson 14** *Mrs. Goose's Baby*

▶ **Comparing and Contrasting**

Directions: Discuss each picture. Have the students write *A* if the picture shows things that are alike and *D* if it shows things that are different.

_____

- - - - - - - - - - - - - - -

_____

COMPREHENSION

Adjectives

Directions: Write the word that describes each picture.

Rule	**Example**
▶ Describing words tell more about something.	▶ A **smart** dog.

sick   big   mad   sad

_____
- - - - - - - - - - - -
_____

_____
- - - - - - - - - - - -
_____

_____
- - - - - - - - - - - -
_____

_____
- - - - - - - - - - - -
_____

▶Adjectives

Practice

Matt is a sad pup.

Min is sick.

Tom is a big cat.

Mom is not mad.

GRAMMAR AND USAGE

Name _____ Date _____

Using Adjectives

Rule	**Example**
▶ Adjectives help describe words.	▶ **Cute** raccoon cubs look like their **caring** parents.

thick   green   hard   long   weak

1. The turtle has a _____ shell.

2. A squirrel has _____ fur.

3. A frog has _____ skin.

4. A mouse has a _____ tail.

5. Kittens have _____ legs.

► **Using Adjectives**

Practice

Directions: Draw a picture of yourself. Write words that describe you.

cute	small	happy	smart
careful	friendly	tall	funny

WRITER'S CRAFT

Types of Sentences

Rule	**Example**
▶ Some sentences tell.	▶ Deer eat grass.
▶ Some sentences ask.	▶ What do toads eat?
▶ Some sentences show strong feeling.	▶ Let's eat!

1. I like to eat bananas

2. Who am I

3. Eagles catch fish

4. Watch out

5. That lion is hungry

Comprehension and Language Arts Skills

▶**Types of Sentences**

Practice

Directions: Listen to each sentence. Put a period, question mark, or exclamation point at the end of each sentence.

6. I have a long neck

7. Who am I

8. Be careful

9. Toads eat worms

10. Yuck

11. Which animals eat insects

GRAMMAR AND USAGE

Main Idea and Details

Directions: Circle the picture that does not belong.

Main Idea: Thanksgiving dinner
Details:

▶ **Main Idea and Details**

Directions: Put an X through the picture that does not belong.

Main idea: A baseball game
Details:

COMPREHENSION

Writing Sentences

Directions: Draw a picture of your favorite food. Then finish each sentence. Put a period, question mark, or exclamation point at the end of each sentence.

Rule

▶ Some sentences tell.

▶ Some sentences ask.

▶ Some sentences show strong feeling.

Example

▶ Deer eat grass.

▶ What do toads eat?

▶ Let's eat!

1. What do I eat _____
   _____
   _ _ _ _ _ _ _ _ _ _ _ _ _

2. I eat _____
   _____
   _ _ _ _ _ _ _ _ _ _ _ _ _

3. I love _____

UNIT 2 Animals • **Lesson 8** *Munch Crunch*

Practice

1. What do snakes eat _____

2. Snakes eat eggs _____

3. They love eggs _____

4. What do eagles eat _____

5. Eagles eat fish _____

6. They love fish _____

WRITER'S CRAFT

Review

Adjectives

| tall | small | long | big |

1. _____
   _____

2. _____
   _____

3. _____
   _____

4. _____
   _____

UNIT 2 Animals • **Lesson II** *Spiders*

►**Review**

►**Types of Sentences**

Directions: Listen to each sentence. Put a period, question mark, or exclamation point at the end of each sentence.

GRAMMAR AND USAGE

5. I like to buzz

6. Who am I

7. I spin a web

8. Who am I

9. Watch out

10. Help, I'm stuck

11. It's time for lunch

12. What happened

UNIT 2 Animals • **Lesson 12** *The Hermit Crab*

Writing Descriptions

Rule
▶ Writers describe things.

Example
▶ Fish can swim fast. They have tails and fins to help them move.

Try It!

Comprehension and Language Arts Skills

▶ **Writing Descriptions**

Practice

Directions: Draw a picture of yourself. Write your name and words to describe you.

WRITER'S CRAFT

_____

- -

_____

_____

- -

_____

Drawing Conclusions

1. Tam and Dan are (not sad, sad).

2. It is (not hot, hot).

3. It is (fun, not fun).

UNIT 2   Animals • **Lesson 14** *The Hermit Crab*

▶ **Drawing Conclusions**

Directions: Read each sentence to students. Have students circle Yes or No to tell whether the sentence is true or not true.

4. The children are at home.   Yes   No

5. They are painting.   Yes   No

6. They are sad.   Yes   No

Possessive Nouns

Rule	**Example**
▶ Add **'s** to a noun or name to show ownership.	▶ Jake**'s** hat dog**'s** tail

1. Pam's car has a flat tire.

2. We are going to Grandma's house.

3. Danny's frog won the race.

4. The bird's eggs are blue.

Possessive Nouns

 Practice

Directions: Write the words that tell who owns each object. The first one is done for you.

5. Sue has an apple.

Sue's apple

6. Joe has a truck.

_____

_ _ _ _ _ _ _ _ _ _ _ _ _ _ _

_____

7. Kate has a ball.

_____

_ _ _ _ _ _ _ _ _ _ _ _ _ _ _

_____

8. The farmer has a hat.

_____

_ _ _ _ _ _ _ _ _ _ _ _ _ _ _

_____

9. Dad bakes a pie.

_____

_ _ _ _ _ _ _ _ _ _ _ _ _ _ _

_____

GRAMMAR AND USAGE

Staying on Topic

Directions: Read the list. Circle the words that stay on topic. Draw a line through the words that do not belong.

Rule

▶ Writers stay on topic. Writers write lists of words that belong together.

Example

▶ Tools for a Carpenter

hammer

saw

drill

ladder

 Try It!

Tools for a Cook

pan

dish

rake

pot

Comprehension and Language Arts Skills

▶ **Staying on Topic**

Practice

| rake | pan | hose | mop | shovel |

Tools for a Gardener

_____

1. _____

2. _____

3. _____

| pen | brush | scissors | drill | comb |

Tools for a Hairdresser

_____

4. _____

5. _____

6. _____

WRITER'S CRAFT

Singular and Plural Nouns

Directions: Read each word next to its picture. Draw a line from each word to its plural.

Rule	**Example**
▶ Add **s** to a noun to show that there is more than one.	▶ bat bat**s** rug rug**s**

1.    car   trucks

2.    train   bikes

3.    truck   cars

4.   bike   trains

UNIT 3 **Things That Go • Lesson 6** *Song of the Train*

▶ **Singular and Plural Nouns**

5. apple _____

_ _ _ _ _ _ _ _ _ _ _ _ _ _ _ _ _ _ _ _

_____

6. dog _____

_ _ _ _ _ _ _ _ _ _ _ _ _ _ _ _ _ _ _ _

_____

7. carrot _____

_ _ _ _ _ _ _ _ _ _ _ _ _ _ _ _ _ _ _ _

_____

8. boat _____

_ _ _ _ _ _ _ _ _ _ _ _ _ _ _ _ _ _ _ _

_____

GRAMMAR AND USAGE

Sensory Details

Directions: Read the sentences. Draw a line under the words that tell how something looks, feels, sounds, smells, and/or tastes.

Rule	**Example**
▶ Writers use words that tell how something looks, feels, sounds, smells, and tastes.	▶ A squirrel has a **long, bushy** tail. **Soft** fur covers its body. Squirrels eat **juicy** berries and **crunchy** nuts. They make **noisy, chirping** sounds.

 **Try It!**

1. A skunk has black fur and a white stripe.

2. Skunks have a stinky spray.

3. Skunks make hissing, growling sounds.

4. They use their strong, sharp claws to dig.

5. Skunks eat soft, chewy worms.

▶ **Sensory Details**

Practice

sharp	long	skinny	squeaky	crunchy

6. A mouse has a _____, _____ tail.

7. They eat _____ seeds.

8. Mice have _____ teeth.

9. Mice make _____ noises.

WRITER'S CRAFT

Comparing and Contrasting

Directions: Circle the thing in each row that is different.

1.

2.   

3.

4.   cdgt   cdgt   cgdt   cdgt

Comparing and Contrasting

Directions: Circle the word or words that tell how the animals are alike.

5.　　　　　four legs　　　　pet

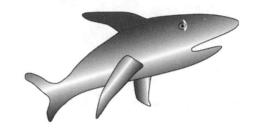

6.　　　　　legs　　　　　　no legs

7.　　　　　live in nest　　　have fur

COMPREHENSION

▶ Review

▶ Possessive Nouns

Directions: Circle the possessive noun that tells who or what has something. Then write who or what owns something on the line. The first one is done for you.

_____

_____

1. The train's whistle is loud.

_____

_____

2. Papa's car is red.

_____

_____

3. Mary's horse runs fast.

_____

_____

4. This is Jason's wagon.

_____

_____

5. Jim's boat has a white sail.

UNIT 3 **Things That Go • Lesson II** *On the Go*

▶ Singular and Plural Nouns

6. snake   snakes

7. pig   pigs

8. ant   ants

9. frog   frogs

10. duck   ducks

11. cow   cows

GRAMMAR AND USAGE

Order Words

Directions: Look at the pictures. Draw a line from the picture to the correct word.

Rule	**Example**
▶ Order words tell the order things happen.	▶ **First** you dig a hole. **Next** you put in a seed. **Then** you cover the seed with dirt. **Last** you water the seed.

Try It!

1.    first

2.    next

3.    last

UNIT 3 **Things That Go • Lesson 14** *Trucks*

▶ Order Words

Practice

Directions: Look at each picture. Write the correct word on the line.

Then	Last	First

4. _____
   _____
   _____ we think of an idea.

5. _____
   _____
   _____ we write.

6. _____
   _____
   _____ we share our writing.

WRITER'S CRAFT

▶Capitalization

Directions: Read each sentence. Circle the word that needs a capital letter.

Rule	**Example**
▶ Days and months begin with capital letters.	▶ **S**unday **J**une

1. Sam and Liz rode bikes on saturday.

2. They went to the park on sunday.

3. School starts on monday, august 29.

4. Sam's birthday is in october.

▶ **Capitalization**

MECHANICS

Practice

Directions: Circle the letter that needs to be a capital. Write the word using a capital letter.

5. monday _____

6. july _____

7. march _____

8. wednesday _____

9. november _____

10. august _____

▶ Classifying

Directions: Draw lines connecting the pairs of objects that belong together.

1.

2.

3.

▶ Classifying

Directions: Draw a line from each animal on the left to the one that is most similar on the right.

4.

5.

6.

7.

COMPREHENSION

Who, What, Where, and When

Rule	Example
▶Writers answer the questions who, what, where, and when to be sure they tell about everything.	Who: **Teachers** are workers. What: They **teach children how to read.** Where: They work **in schools.** When: They work **all day long.**

Try It!

1. The man    when

2. mops the floor    where

3. every night   who

4. at the shop.    what

▶ **Who, What, Where, and When**

Practice

Directions: Read each sentence. Look at the underlined words. Write the question word that it answers.

| who | what | where | when |

5. We mail letters at a <u>post office</u>.

_____

- -

_____

6. The post office opens <u>in the morning</u>.

_____

- -

_____

7. Workers <u>sort the letters</u>.

_____

- -

_____

8. A <u>letter carrier</u> brings mail to your house.

_____

- -

_____

WRITER'S CRAFT

End Punctuation

Directions: Read each sentence. Draw a line to the correct end mark.

Rule	**Example**
▶ Sentences end with . or ? or !	▶ Where is the moon? It is in the sky. See how big it looks!

1. Who has a dog

2. Tomás has a dog

3. The dog is bigger than Tomás

!

?

.

4. Where is the frog

5. The frog is on the log

6. Hop away frog

.

?

!

▶ **End Punctuation**

Practice

Directions: Read each sentence. Write the correct end marks.

7. Today I will ride a bus _____

8. Where will the bus go _____

9. It is the first day of school _____

10. I am excited _____

11. I like school _____

12. How do you get to school _____

MECHANICS

A Friendly Letter

Directions: Circle the date with a blue crayon. Circle the greeting in red. Circle the message in green. Circle the closing in black. Circle the writer's name in brown.

▶Friendly letters have five parts.

Date	June 19, 2001
Greeting	Dear Amy,
Message	We saw the Liberty Bell. It weighs more than a ton! It has a crack. They don't ring it anymore.
Closing	Your friend,
Your Name	Jennifer

 **Try It!**

March 2, 2004

Dear Joe,
   My school had a book sale. I got three new books. Would you like to read my books?

                    Your friend,
                    Ellie

▶ **A Friendly Letter**

Practice

We went to Fort Clatsop.   May 12, 2002
The rangers showed us how candles and
shoes were made.
We watched them build a boat!
Your friend,   Drew   Dear Pat,

WRITER'S CRAFT

Review

Capitalization

_____

1. Rose has a birthday in may.   _____

2. Her party is friday.   _____

3. january is the coldest month.   _____

4. It rains a lot in april.   _____

5. We have music class on tuesday.   _____

6. On thursday we go to art class.   _____

UNIT 4 **Our Neighborhood at Work • Lesson 11** *Worksong*

▶ **End Punctuation**   ▶ **Review**

Directions: Read the story. Write the correct end marks.

MECHANICS

I like to walk down my street _____ Would

you like to walk with me _____ I can see flowers

and trees _____ Who moved into the red house _____

Maybe a new friend lives there _____ Friends are

nice _____ That was a long walk _____ Thank you

for walking with me _____ I am tired _____

Comprehension and Language Arts Skills   **UNIT 4 • Lesson 11**   **57**

Audience and Purpose

Rule

▶Writers think about who is going to read their writing. They think about what they want to tell.

Example

▶A coach writes game rules for the players.
▶A teacher writes a note to a parent.
▶A boy writes an invitation to invite friends to a party.

Try It!

1. someone who gave a gift   tell them about your report

2. your class   write about your feelings

3. your parent   write a story about your family

4. yourself   thank them for a gift

▶ **Audience and Purpose**

Practice

WRITER'S CRAFT

Directions: Read each purpose for writing. Write the audience on the line. The audience is the person who will read the writing.

teacher friend librarian yourself pet store owner

5. journal page _____

6. invitation to a party _____

7. report about plants _____

8. questions about dogs _____

9. list of books _____

Longer Sentences

Directions: Read each sentence. Draw a line under the words that tell how, when, or where.

Rule

▶Writers write longer sentences to tell more. They write words that tell how, when, and where.

Example

▶Eagles eat fish.

How: Eagles eat fish **quickly.**

When: Eagles eat fish **often.**

Where: Eagles eat fish **out of** the water.

1. Otters swim fast.

2. Otters slide down muddy hills.

3. Otters play every day.

UNIT 4 Our Neighborhood at Work • **Lesson 14** *Worksong*

▶**Longer Sentences**

Practice

| on my lap | softly | sometimes |

My cat purrs.

How: **4.** My cat purrs _____ .

When: **5.** My cat purrs _____ .

Where: **6.** My cat purrs _____ .

| in the sky | every day | quickly |

Birds fly.

How: **7.** Birds fly _____ .

When: **8.** Birds fly _____ .

Where: **9.** Birds fly _____ .

WRITER'S CRAFT

Adjectives

Rule	**Example**
▶ Adjectives are words used to describe nouns.	▶ The dog is *big.* That is a *big* dog.

Try It!

1. The pan is hot.

2. The gray whales swim.

3. Sam has a yellow ball.

4. We filled the big pot.

▶**Adjectives**

Practice

| new | tall | three | gold | wet |

Directions: Read each sentence. Write the adjective that describes each picture on the line. Use the words in the box.

5. The ___*three*___ mice run away.

6. Becky's coat has ___*gold*___ buttons.

7. There are ___*tall*___ buildings in the city.

8. Dan took off his ___*wet*___ shoes.

9. I rode my ___*new*___ bike in the park.

GRAMMAR AND USAGE

Main Idea and Details

Main Idea: Day at the Beach
Details:

► **Main Idea and Details**

Main Idea: Nighttime
Details:

Directions: Put an X through the picture that does not belong.

Order Words

Rule

▶ Order words tell the order things happen.

Example

▶ **First,** the batter holds the bat.

Next, the pitcher throws the ball.

Then, the batter swings the bat.

Last, the batter hits the ball and runs to first base.

 **Try It!**

1. First, the runner stretches.

2. Then, she goes to the starting line.

3. Next, she waits to hear the starting bell.

4. Last, she starts running.

UNIT 5 Weather • **Lesson 3** *When a Storm Comes Up*

▶ **Order Words**

Practice

Directions: Read the sentences. Write the order word on the line.

Next	First	Last	Then

_____

5. _____, Matt makes a sandwich.

_____

6. _____, he wraps it in plastic.

_____

7. _____, he gets an apple and raisins.

_____

8. _____, he puts everything in a bag.

▶Verbs

Rule	Example
▶ Verbs show action.	▶ We **walk** to school. She **rides** the bus.

spins	run	smiles	talk

1. smiles

2. run

3. spins

4. talt

UNIT 5   Weather • **Lesson 6** *Listen to the Rain*

▶ **Verbs**

GRAMMAR AND USAGE

Practice

Directions: Read the sentences. Circle the word that shows action in each sentence.

5. A tree (grows) in the yard.

6. The wind (blows) the branches.

7. Leaves (fall) from the tree.

8. Dad (rakes) the leaves.

9. Jake (helps) Kayla.

10. The children (put) the leaves in the bag.

▶ Review

▶ **Adjectives**

Directions: Read each sentence. Draw a line under the words that describe a noun. Circle the noun that they describe.

1. My family takes fun trips.

2. I put on my new boots.

3. We climbed a steep hill.

4. Dad made a tasty lunch.

5. We sat by a big old tree.

Name _____ Date _____

▶ **Verbs**   ▶ **Review**

Directions: Read the words in the box. Choose the verb that fits each sentence. Write the verb on the line.

| wins | kicks | runs | cheers | ties |

_____

6. Joshua _____ his shoe.

7. Ashley _____ the ball.

8. She _____ down the field.

9. The crowd _____ .

10. Our team _____ the game!

Comprehension and Language Arts Skills   UNIT 5 • Lesson II   **71**

Commas in a Series

Directions: Read each sentence. Write the commas where they belong.

Rule	Example
▶ Commas are used in lists of three or more.	▶ Lauren, Nathan, and Trevor are in my class.

Try It!

1. Mom Dad and I went to the store.

2. We bought milk eggs butter and flour.

3. I helped Mom measure pour and mix the batter.

4. Dad and I rinsed washed and dried the dishes.

5. We ate pancakes with fruit milk and juice.

► **Commas in a Series**

MECHANICS

Practice

Shane Ryan and Amber went to camp. The camp had a lake trees and hills. The children played soccer baseball and basketball. They also liked to hike swim and sing songs. It was a fun happy and busy week.

Classifying

Directions: Write the word that goes with each object.

truck	bird	bee
jet	car	bike

wheels

wings

1. _____

4. _____

2. _____

5. _____

3. _____

6. _____

UNIT 6 Journeys • **Lesson 2** *Captain Bill Pinkney's Journey*

▶ **Classifying**

Directions: Choose two words that belong together and write them on the lines.

| sock | brush | cookies | foot |
| milk | bat | comb | ball |

7. _____   _____

8. _____   _____

9. _____   _____

10. _____   _____

A Paragraph That Explains

Rule

▶Writers use paragraphs to explain. The first sentence tells what the writer will explain. The other sentences tell what happens in the correct order.

Try It!

1. ____ Last the robin pulls the worm out of the ground.

2. ____ A robin eats worms.

3. ____ First the robin walks on the grass.

4. ____ Next the robin stops walking.

5. ____ Then the robin hears a worm.

UNIT 6 Journeys • **Lesson 3** *Captain Bill Pinkney's Journey*

▶**A Paragraph That Explains**

Practice

First I get a can of dog food.
Then I open the can.
Next I pour the food in the dish.
Last my dog eats.

_____

_____

_____

_____

_____

_____

_____

_____

_____

_____

_____

_____

WRITER'S CRAFT

Capitalization: Cities and States

Directions: Circle the names of the cities and states that are capitalized correctly.

Rule	**Example**
▸ The names of cities and states always begin with a capital letter.	▸ Madison, Wisconsin

Try It!

1. Columbus, Ohio
   columbus, ohio

2. Reno, Nevada
   reno, nevada

3. austin, texas
   Austin, Texas

4. Springfield, Illinois
   springfield, Illinois

**Capitalization:
Cities and States**

MECHANICS

Practice

Directions: Read each sentence. Underline the word or words that should begin with a capital letter. Write the capital letters above the words.

5. The Statue of Liberty is in new york.

6. Yellowstone National Park is in wyoming.

7. The Sears Tower in chicago is the tallest building in the world.

8. The Space Needle in seattle was left after a world's fair.

9. Our national anthem was written in baltimore, Maryland.

10. In arizona you can visit the Grand Canyon.

Place and Location Words

Directions: Look at each picture. Draw a line to the words that tell where.

Rule	Example
▶ Writers use words that tell exactly where people, places, and things are.	▶ The duck is **in** the water. This bridge is **over** the water. The table is **behind** the cat.

 Try It!

1.    on the log

2.    in the nest

3.    beside the fishbowl

► **Place and Location Words**

Practice

| over   on   between   under   in   behind |

_____
- - - - - - -
4. The squirrel sits _____ the log.

_____
- - - - - - -
5. A cat walks _____ the dishes.

_____
- - - - - - -
6. The dog stands _____ the fence.

_____
- - - - - - -
7. The gerbil hides _____ the paper.

_____
- - - - - - -
8. The jellyfish swims _____ the shell.

_____
- - - - - - -
9. A bird finds a worm _____ a tree.

WRITER'S CRAFT

UNIT 6 Journeys • **Lesson II** *The Special Day*

Making Inferences

_____

- -

_____

- -

_____

- -

_____

- -

_____

- -

_____

UNIT 6 Journeys • **Lesson II** *The Special Day*

▶ **Making Inferences**

Directions: Look at the picture. Based on what is in the picture, write three sentences describing what is happening. Answers will vary.

_____

- -

_____

- -

_____

- -

_____

- -

_____

- -

_____

COMPREHENSION

▷Review

▶Commas in a Series

Directions: Read each sentence. Write the commas where they belong.

1. I went to the beach with Uncle Tim Aunt Ann and my cousin Scott.

2. I brought my shovel pail and sand toys.

3. Scott and I played in the soft clean white sand.

4. Aunt Ann brought grapes cherries and plums for snacks.

5. We swam played and listened to the waves all day long.

6. Everyone was hot tired and happy.

UNIT 6 Journeys • **Lesson 11** *That Special Day*

▶ **Capitalization: Cities and States**

Directions: Read each sentence. Draw a line under the 10 words that name cities and states that should begin with a capital letter. Write the correct capital letter above the word.

1. Pete lives in grove city, Ohio.

2. His grandma lives in columbia, maryland.

3. Pete's family drives through pennsylvania to get to Grandma's house.

4. Pete's cousin lives in oak park, Illinois.

5. Pete's family drives through indiana to get to his cousin's house.

6. Next winter everyone will go skiing in vail, colorado.

MECHANICS

Form of a Paragraph

Directions: Read the paragraph. Draw a line through the sentence that does not belong.

Rule	Example
▶ Writers use sentences that go together to write a paragraph. 	▶ Helicopters are used to help people. They carry hurt people to hospitals. They take food to places people can't go. They can take heavy equipment to a rooftop. Helicopters are very useful.

 **Try It!**

Trains have many cars. Sleeper cars have beds where people can sleep. Dining cars are where people can eat. We ate carrots for dinner. Coaches are cars where people can sit and look out the windows. A train has cars for all the passengers.

▶ **Form of a Paragraph**

Practice

A bike has many parts.
A bike has a seat.
It has two wheels.
It has handlebars.
I ride the bus to school.
All parts of a bike work together.
A car has four wheels.

A bike has many

parts.

WRITER'S CRAFT

Past Tense Verbs

Rule

▶ Add *-ed* to a verb to show that something already happened.

▶ Some verbs change to show that something already happened. They don't use *-ed*.

Example

▶ Yesterday I **walked** with Lisa.

▶ Cara sings a song. Yesterday she **sang** a song.

Try It!

Look at each picture. Circle the verb that tells that it already happened.

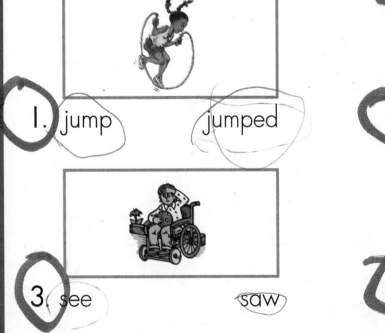

1. jump   jumped

2. clap   clapped

3. see   saw

4. eat   ate

▶ **Past Tense Verbs**

Practice

Read the sentence. Write the verb that tells that something already happened.

5. Billy and I _____*went*_____ to the fair.

go   went

6. Billy _____*played*_____ games.

played   plays

7. He _____*pinned*_____ the tail on the donkey.

pin   pinned

8. We _____*saw*_____ a clown.

saw   see

GRAMMAR AND USAGE

Comprehension and Language Arts Skills   UNIT 7 • Lesson I   **89**

Exact Words

Rule	Example
▶Writers write exact words to help readers understand. 	▶A **honeybee hovers** over the **bright yellow** flower. Its **long, skinny** tongue **sucks** up **sweet** nectar.

 **Try It!**

Read the sentence. Draw a line under the exact words.

1. The dragonfly's shiny, blue body sparkles in the bright sunlight.

2. Its four, long wings flutter rapidly.

3. It skims across the quiet pond.

4. You hear a soft rattle as the beautiful dragonfly darts here and there.

▶ **Exact Words**

WRITER'S CRAFT

Practice

Look at the picture. Write exact words
that tell about it.

_____

- -

_____

_____

- -

_____

_____

- -

_____

_____

- -

_____

_____

- -

_____

Cause and Effect

Read each sentence. Circle the best
cause, **a** or **b**.

1. Jenny ran and grabbed a paper towel.
   - **a.** She had spilled some juice.
   - **b.** She needed to write a note.

2. Tom blew out all six candles on the cake.
   - **a.** He was afraid of fire.
   - **b.** It was his birthday.

3. Dad bought a new rake.
   - **a.** The old rake was broken.
   - **b.** He liked its blue color.

4. Mom took Shane to the dentist.
   - **a.** He had a chipped tooth.
   - **b.** It was on the way to the store.

▶**Cause and Effect**

Match the effects and causes.

Effects	**Causes**
5. Everyone cheered.	She was thirsty.
6. There was a thunderstorm.	We had run out of gas.
7. Mom gave Amy some juice.	Andy won the race.
8. Our car suddenly stopped.	It was too heavy for her.
9. Barbara carried the box for Meg.	The sky became very dark.
10. We warmed our hands by the campfire.	She needed to wrap a package.
11. Mom handed Georgia some tape.	It was so cold.

COMPREHENSION

Pronouns

Rule	Example
▶ A pronoun takes the place of a noun.	▶ Sam poured the juice. **He** poured **it**.

Try It!

Look at the picture. Read the sentence.
Write the correct pronoun on the line.

| it | they | we | ~~he~~ | him | ~~she~~ | I |

1. I can kick __it__ very far.

2. __She__ is on my team.

3. __He__ is my coach.

UNIT 7 Keep Trying • **Lesson 3** *The Kite*

▶**Pronouns**

Practice

Read each pair of sentences. Write the correct pronoun in the blank.

she	he	her	them	I

4. My name is Kim.

   _____ am seven years old.

5. Janet likes to paint.

   _____ is an artist.

6. Chad lives next door.

   _____ likes to draw.

7. Janet and Chad are going to an art show.

   I am going with _____ .

GRAMMAR AND USAGE

UNIT 7   Keep Trying • **Lesson 3** *The Kite*

Staying on Topic

Rule	**Example**
▶Writers stay on the topic. 	▶ I wanted to learn how to ride a bike. Every time I tried to ride, I fell. I wanted to quit. Then my brother helped me. Now I can ride my bike!

 **Try It!**

Read the paragraph. Draw a line through the sentence that does not belong.

I wrote a story about my friend Jen. I told about the time she helped me paint a picture. She has three cats. I read my story to the class.

▶**Staying on Topic**

Practice

Write a paragraph using the sentences
that stay on topic.

My family visited the Grand Canyon.
We walked on the trails.
I have new shoes.
We rode a raft down the river.
My sister is nine.
We rode horses.
The Grand Canyon is a fun place to go.

WRITER'S CRAFT

_____

- -

_____

- -

_____

- -

_____

- -

_____

Drawing Conclusions

Look at the picture. Complete each sentence by circling the best word.

1. The children are (playing, working).

2. It is (winter, summer).

3. The children are having (fun, no fun).

▶ **Drawing Conclusions**

COMPREHENSION

Look at the picture. Find the best
answer. Circle **a, b,** or **c.**

4. Joy is smiling because:

　ⓐ She has an ice-cream cone.

　b. She just went to the doctor.

　c. She is petting a dog.

5. Min is upset because:

　a. She is going to the park.

　ⓑ She feels sick.

　c. She lost her doll.

Possessive Pronouns

Rule	**Example**
▶ A possessive pronoun takes the place of a possessive noun. It shows ownership.	▶ Ty's shoes are black. **Her** shoes are black.

Read each sentence. Circle the correct possessive pronoun. Write it on the line.

1. I live in a house on Maple Street.

_____

_ _ _ _ _ _

_____ house is green.   My   Its

2. Grandma is bringing a puppy.

_____

_ _ _ _ _ _

_____ name is Max.   Her   Its

UNIT 7 Keep Trying • **Lesson 4** *The Garden*

▶**Possessive Pronouns**

Practice

Look at the picture. Read the sentence.
Write the possessive pronoun and what
is owned.

my	your	her	his	its

3. Maria has a book. _____

4. Kin has a ball. _____

5. The cat has a tail. _____

6. I have a balloon. _____

7. You have an apple. _____

Sentences

Rule	Example
▶Writers write complete sentences. A sentence has a naming part and an action part. Every sentence begins with a capital letter and ends with an end mark.	▶Raindrops splash on the ground. A lot of rain makes a mud puddle.

Draw a line to match the sentence parts to make a complete sentence.

1. The sun   blow.

2. Snowflakes   rumbles.

3. Strong winds   shines.

4. Thunder   fall.

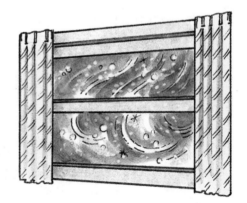

▶**Sentences**

Practice

Look at the picture. Write words that complete each sentence.

_____

5. Sam and Liz _____

_____

6. _____ was a sunny day.

_____

7. Sam's bike _____

_____

8. _____ rode to the school.

Main Idea and Details

Read the main idea. Circle the picture
that does not belong.

Main Idea: Nature/Plants
Details:

▶ **Main Idea and Details**

Read the main idea. Put an **X** on the picture that does not belong.

Main Idea: Insects
Details:

Adjectives That Compare

Rule

▶ Add *-er* to a describing word to compare two things. Add *-est* to a describing word to compare more than two things.

Example

▶ I am **older** than my brother. Mom is the **oldest** in our family.

 **Try It!**

Add *-er* and *-est* to make describing words that compare.

_____

1. tall _____

_____

2. short _____

_____

3. fast _____

_____

4. slow _____

▶ **Adjectives That Compare**

Practice

Read each sentence. Write the correct word on the line.

5. Henry is _____ than Fran.
   taller   tallest

6. Fran has the _____ hair of all.
   longer   longest

7. I am the _____ person in my class.
   taller   tallest

8. Fran's cat is _____ than Henry's fish.
   big   bigger

9. My dog is the _____ pet of all.
   bigger   biggest

GRAMMAR AND USAGE

Longer Sentences

> **Rule**
>
> ▶Writers write longer sentences to tell more. They use words that tell how, where, and when.
>
>
>
> **Example**
>
> ▶Stars shine.
> How: Stars shine **brightly.**
> When: Stars shine at **night.**
> Where: Stars shine **everywhere.**

 **Try It!**

Read the sentences. Circle the words that tell how, when, or where.

1. The plane lands perfectly.

2. The plane lands at the airport.

3. The plane lands soon.

▶**Longer Sentences**

Practice

Read the sentence. Use the words in the box to make the sentence longer.
Truck drivers travel.

| around the country   every week   safely |

4. How: _____

_____

_____

_____

5. When: _____

_____

_____

_____

6. Where: _____

_____

_____

_____

WRITER'S CRAFT

UNIT 7   Keep Trying • **Lesson 7** *The Hare and the Tortoise*

▶ Sequence

Put the sentences in order. Use 1–4.

_____

_____ Jan and Pete wake up.

_____

_____ Then Pete and Jan leave for school.

_____

_____ Jan puts on her coat.

_____

_____ Pete brushes his teeth.

► **Sequence**

Put the sentences in order using 1–6.

_____

_____ Jill gave the cat some food.

_____

_____ The cat woke Jill up in the morning.

_____

_____ Jill went outside to play.

_____

_____ After breakfast Jill got dressed and
_____ put on her shoes.

_____

_____ After the cat ate some food, it sat
_____ on Jill's lap while she ate her cereal.

_____

_____ Jill's mother asked her to come
_____ inside for dinner.

▷ Review

▶ Past Tense Verbs

Read each sentence. Circle the word
that tells what happened in the past.

1. My ball rolled away.

2. I looked for it all day.

3. I crawled under the bed.

4. I climbed over the chair.

5. I ran down the stairs.

6. Then I opened the door.

7. I found my ball!

UNIT 7 Keep Trying • **Lesson 7** *The Hare and the Tortoise*

Pronouns, Possessive Pronouns, and Adjectives That Compare

▶ **Review**

Read the paragraph. Draw a box around the possessive pronouns. Circle the other pronouns. Underline the three adjectives that compare.

I you we they us it her my

Grant Park has the tallest trees in town. I went to the park with my friend. Her name is Amy. The park was a mess. We wanted to clean it up. We saw my friends Jake and Luke. They are older than I am. They helped us pick up trash in the park. Now it is the cleanest park in town.

GRAMMAR AND USAGE

Dialogue

Rule	**Example**
▶The exact words a character speaks are called dialogue. Write quotation marks at the beginning and end of the exact words someone says.	▶Jake asked, "Who was Johnny Appleseed?" Mr. Foster replied, "He was a pioneer who planted many apple trees."

 Read the sentence. Draw a line under the words that are said. Draw a circle around who is speaking.

1. "I read a book about Benjamin Franklin," said Pat.

2. "He invented a new kind of glasses," said Aaron.

3. "He also invented the heating stove," added Pat.

▶ **Dialogue**

Practice

Write quotation marks at the beginning and end of the words someone says.

4. I think I'll write a make-believe story, said Randy.

5. Are you going to write a scary story? asked Devin.

6. Why don't you write a story about a spaceship? asked Michelle.

7. No, I think I'll write about an animal that can talk, answered Randy.

8. That's a good idea, said Michelle.

9. You could write about a talking skunk! exclaimed Devin.

10. Or you could write about a talking lizard! added Michelle.

WRITER'S CRAFT

Kinds of Sentences

Rule	Example
▶ A sentence that tells something ends with a period.	▶ I hit the ball.
▶ A sentence that asks something ends with a question mark.	▶ How far did it go?
▶ A sentence that shows strong feeling ends with an exclamation point.	▶ I hit a home run!

 Read each sentence. Write the end mark that goes with each kind of sentence.

1. I like to play games _____

2. What is your favorite game _____

3. I love checkers _____

UNIT 8 Games • **Lesson I** *Unit Introduction*

► **Kinds of Sentences**

Practice

4. Circle the telling sentence.

Who ran in the race?

I ran in the race.

5. Circle the asking sentence.

Cara plays soccer.

Did you see her play?

6. Circle the sentence that shows strong feeling.

My dad is proud of me.

He gave me a big hug!

Sequence

Circle the word that tells about time.

1. They must leave for school (now.)

2. We can play (after) we do the dishes.

3. Beth sang (as) Chuck played the guitar.

4. The calf stayed in the barn (during) the storm.

5. Kevin fed our cat (while) we went on a trip.

6. Grandpa will arrive very (soon.)

7. Sam washed the car (before) he left.

8. Tina has grown an inch (since) June.

UNIT 8   Games • **Lesson 2** *A Game Called Piggle*

▶ Sequence

Look at the picture. Put the sentences in order. Use 1–4.

3 _____ Soon he is at the pond.

1 _____ The turtle wakes up as the sun rises.

4 _____ Then he slips into the water.

2 _____ Slowly he walks along the path until he reaches the pond.

COMPREHENSION

Sensory Details

Rule	Example
▶ Writers use words that tell how something looks, feels, sounds, smells, and tastes. Writers want readers to have good clear pictures in their minds.	▶ I walked on the **old wooden** bridge. ▶ **Cool** water flows in the river.

 Draw a line under the words that tell how something looks, feels, sounds, tastes, or smells.

1. The ring had a beautiful, sparkling stone.

2. Do you hear the horse's clomping hooves?

3. Crisp, warm popcorn makes a good snack.

4. Wear a heavy coat on the cold, damp mornings.

▶**Sensory Details**

Practice

Write words to finish the sentences.

| sandy | cool | bumpy | fluffy | white | colorful |

5. We walked on the ___sandy___ beach.

6. We swam in the ___cool___ water.

7. We picked up ___bumpy___,

___colorful___ shells.

8. We looked up at the ___white___,
___fluffy___ clouds.

WRITER'S CRAFT

Comparing and Contrasting

Look at each picture. Circle the phrase
that tells about the pictures.

1. (things to eat)   fruits and vegetables

2. three pictures of girls   (people drinking from cups)

UNIT 8 Games • **Lesson 3** *Jafta*

▶ **Comparing and Contrasting**

Look at each picture. Circle the phrase
that tells about the pictures.

3. things that grow   plants with flowers

4. animals with fur   animals with teeth

5. animals that live on farms   things that people can ride

Comprehension and Language Arts Skills   UNIT 8 • Lesson 3   **123**

Sentence Parts

Rule	Example
▶ Every sentence has two parts. The **naming part** tells who or what. The **action part** tells what the naming part does.	▶ The crowd watches the game. naming part action part

Try It! Read each sentence. Draw a line under the naming part. Circle the action part.

1. The children play a game.

2. David plays with marbles.

3. Paula puts a puzzle together.

4. All the children help clean the room.

▶ **Sentence Parts**

Practice

Draw a line from each naming part to the correct action part to make a complete sentence.

5. The ball   win the game.

6. Maggie   runs fast.

7. Ben   bounces.

8. The players   throws her ball to James.

Name _Boy on 5/7/6?_ Date _____

▶ Contractions

Rule	**Example**
▶ Words can be shortened to make contractions. Some letters are taken out. An (') takes the place of missing letters.	▶ was not **wasn't** The (') takes the place of the **o** in **not**.

 **Try It!** Write the contraction on the line.

isn't	I'll	we're	can't

1. I will _I'll_

2. cannot _can't_

3. we are _we're_

Comprehension and Language Arts Skills

UNIT 8   Games • **Lesson 6**   *The Great Ball Game*

▶ **Contractions**

Practice

Read each sentence. The underlined words can be shortened. Write the contraction on the line.

it's   She's   hasn't   aren't   don't   we'll

4. We <u>do not</u> like the rain.

5. <u>We will</u> play a game.

6. Cory <u>has not</u> played the game.

7. Now <u>it is</u> Amy's turn.

8. <u>She is</u> a good player.

9. They <u>are not</u> going outside today.

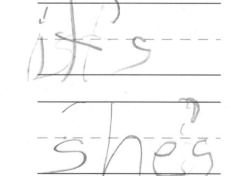

don't

we'll

hasn't

it's

she's

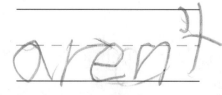

aren't

GRAMMAR AND USAGE

Comprehension and Language Arts Skills   **UNIT 8 • Lesson 6**   **127**

UNIT 8 Games • **Lesson 6** *The Great Ball Game*

Repeating Sounds

Rule	Example
▶ Writers use words that begin with the same sound.	▶ Sea waves **s**plashed and **s**plattered on the **s**eashore. ▶ **C**ats **c**url up on **c**uddly **c**ushions.

 **Try It!** Read the sentence. Circle the words that begin with repeating sounds.

1. Whirling wind whisks the white snow into the air.

2. Seth sleds down the slippery, snowy slope.

3. Bob bounces behind his brother.

4. Greta giggles and gasps as she gallops.

▶ **Repeating Sounds**

Practice

Draw a picture showing something you like to do. Write a sentence to tell about it. Use words that begin with repeating sounds.

WRITER'S CRAFT

_____

- -

_____

_____

- -

_____

- -

_____

Cause and Effect

Read each effect. Circle the best cause,
a or **b**.

1. Pam's new coat is all dirty.
   a. It always looks dirty.
   b. She dropped it in a mud puddle.

2. Tree branches were all over the ground.
   a. A strong wind blew that day.
   b. Birds were building their nests.

3. Mark's white socks are now pink.
   a. Someone played a trick on him.
   b. They were washed with something red.

4. Tammy's bike has a flat tire.
   a. She ran over a nail.
   b. She rode it too much.

5. The puppy was all wet.
   a. It had spilled its water dish.
   b. It had been out in the rain.

UNIT 8 Games • **Lesson 7** *The Big Team Relay Race*

▶**Cause and Effect**

Match the sentences that go together.

Effects	**Causes**
6. Margo runs to the field.	The people moved away.
7. Kevin called his grandmother.	It was raining.
8. Sam could not open the lock.	He wanted to wish her a happy birthday.
9. Paula could not find her book.	She is late for soccer practice.
10. That house is empty.	She left it at school.
11. Carol grabbed an umbrella.	Her friend had come to visit her.
12. Sue ran to the door.	Her shoes were too small.
13. Alice's feet hurt.	He had the wrong key.

UNIT 8 Games • **Lesson 7** *The Big Team Relay Race*

Review

▶ **Kinds of Sentences**

Read each sentence. Draw a line to the
end mark for each kind of sentence.

1. It is so cold   ?

2. We are building a snowman   !

3. Do you like to play in the snow   .

▶ **Sentence Parts**

Draw a line from each naming part
to the correct action part to make a
complete sentence.

4. My hat   melted.

5. Nicole   fell off my head.

6. The snowman   slipped on the ice.

UNIT 8 Games • **Lesson 7** *The Big Team Relay Race*

▶**Contractions**   ▶**Review**

Draw a line from each pair of words to the correct contraction.

7. she is   we've

8. we have   doesn't

9. does not   she's

Write the correct contraction.

We're	She's	It's	don't

_____

10. _____ my best friend.

_____

11. I _____ do anything without my friend.

_____

12. _____ in the same class.

_____

13. _____ nice to have a friend.

GRAMMAR AND USAGE

Organizing a Paragraph That Describes

Rule	Example
▶ Writers use paragraphs to describe objects, people, and places. The first sentence tells what the writer will describe. The other sentences describe it.	▶ Many playgrounds have swings. The frame is made of metal. Two long chains hang from the top steel bar. At the bottom of the chains there is a heavy plastic seat. Swings are a fun thing on a playground.

 **Try It!**   Read the paragraph. Circle the sentence that should be first.

Then there is a long ramp from the top to the bottom. It has a metal ladder to climb. Slides are fun if you like to go up and down. Our playground has a slide. At the top there are two curved handlebars.

► **Organizing a Paragraph that Describes**

Practice

Look at the picture. Write sentences
to finish the paragraph.

An owl is my
favorite kind of bird.

_____

- - - - - - - - - - - - - - - - -

_____

_____

- - - - - - - - - - - - - - - - -

_____

_____

- - - - - - - - - - - - - - - - -

_____

_____

- - - - - - - - - - - - - - - - -

_____

WRITER'S CRAFT

▶Review

▶Nouns

Read each sentence. Find and circle nine nouns.

1. Dillon and Kailey live on a farm.

2. The children feed the chickens.

3. The chickens eat corn.

4. Kailey counts the yellow chicks.

Name _____ 5/31/07 _____ Date _____

▶ Pronouns   ▶ Review

Read each sentence. Write the sentence using the pronouns at the left.

| They / it | 5. Sonya and Robert found a pail. |

~~They~~ found it.

| it / She | 6. Sonya put sand in the pail. |

She put sand in it.

| He / her | 7. Robert helped Sonya build a castle. |

he helped her.

| him / She | 8. Sonya thanked Robert. |

she thanked him

Drawing Conclusions

Look at each picture. Then answer each question. Circle your answers.

1. How does Sue feel?
   a. well   **b.** not well

2. Why does she feel this way?
   a. She ate too much.
   b. The ride made her dizzy.
   c. The ride was too slow.

3. How does Christy feel?
   a. sad   **b.** proud

4. Why does she feel this way?
   a. She grew the biggest pumpkin.
   b. The judge is smiling.
   c. She is at the fair.

▶ **Drawing Conclusions**

Read the story. Answer each question with an X. Follow the directions under each question.

   Pam rubbed her hands while looking up and down the street. She pulled her coat around her and put her hands in her pockets. Sitting on the bench, Pam shivered and waited.

5. Where is Pam? inside _____ outside _____

Draw a line under the words in the story that tell you this.

6. What is it like outside? cold _____ warm _____

Draw circles around the words in the story that tell you this.

COMPREHENSION

End Rhyme

Rule	**Example**
▶ A rhyming poem has rhyming words at the end of each line.	▶ A red and green **bug** Creeps across the **rug!**

 **Try It!**

Read the poems. Draw a circle around the rhyming words.

1. A bushy tailed fox
   Jumped out of the box.

2. Hear bells ring,
   Hear birds sing,
   While you swing!

UNIT 9 Being Afraid • **Lesson 2** *My Brother Is Afraid of Just About Everything*

▶**End Rhyme**

Practice

Read the poems. Write the rhyming words on the lines.

| grab | line | sun | splashes |

3. On the sand walks a crab

_____

- - - - - - - - - - -

With its claws ready to _____!

4. A big wave crashes _____

- - - - - - - - - - -

And then it _____!

5. I counted nine

_____

- - - - - - - - - -

Ducks in a _____.

6. Three mice run

_____

- - - - - - - - -

In the warm _____.

▷Review

▶Verbs

Read the verbs in the box. Choose the verb that fits each sentence. Write the verb on the line.

climb	rakes	write	jumps

_____

1. Sally _____ rope.

2. I can _____ my name.

3. Dad _____ the leaves.

4. Mike and Adam _____ trees.

UNIT 9 Being Afraid • **Lesson 3** *Little Miss Muffet*

▶**Verbs**

▶**Review**

Read the sentences. Circle the verb in each sentence.

5. Dad cooks the meat.

6. Mom opens the basket.

7. Tommy drinks his juice.

8. Alice reads a book.

9. Aunt Marie watches Tommy.

10. I hide behind the bush.

GRAMMAR AND USAGE

Review

Kinds of Sentences

Draw a line under the telling sentence.
Circle the asking sentence. Draw a box
around the strong feeling sentence.

1. Where is the cheese?

2. The mouse ate the cheese!

3. I like cheese.

▶**End Marks**   ▶**Review**

Write the correct end mark after each sentence.

4. We are going to Aunt Sue's house

5. Where does she live

6. Aunt Sue lives in Ohio

7. Can we bring our puppy

8. Aunt Sue just loves puppies

GRAMMAR, USAGE, AND MECHANICS

Comparing and Contrasting

What is the group of sentences about?
Circle your answers.

1. Suzy is happy, because it is her birthday.

2. Todd is upset, because his toy truck is broken.

3. John is sad because it is raining, and he cannot go outside to play.

feelings	the weather

1. People eat apples and bananas.

2. Horses eat oats and grass.

3. Birds eat seeds and worms.

plants	eating

► **Comparing and Contrasting**

COMPREHENSION

Circle the word that is different.

1. cat   cat   coat   cat

2. worm   warm   worm   worm

3. big   big   big   bag

4. boy   toy   toy   toy

5. read   read   read   reed

6. quick   quick   quack   quick

7. clue   cue   clue   clue

8. blew   blue   blew   blew

9. knot   not   not   not

10. plain   plain   plane   plain

▷Review

▷Adjectives

Read each sentence. Draw a line under the words that describe a noun. Circle the noun that they describe. The first one is done for you.

1. It is a cold snowy day.

2. The big yellow dog runs in the snow.

3. Marcy has a fuzzy green hat.

4. Matthew wears his black gloves.

5. The children like to play in the fluffy white snow.

6. They come inside for a hot drink.

7. Marcy and Matthew sit by the cozy warm fire.

8. The tired children get ready for bed.

UNIT 9   Being Afraid • **Lesson 7** *The Cat and the Mice*

Adjectives That Compare

Read each sentence. Write the correct adjective that compares in the blank.

9. Today is the _____ day of the year.

    colder   coldest

10. Dan's coat is _____ than mine.

    warm   warmer

11. We made a _____ snowman than Paul.

    biggest   bigger

12. Joan made the _____ snowman in town.

    biggest   bigger

GRAMMAR AND USAGE

Cause and Effect

Read each effect. Circle the best cause,
a or **b**.

1. Mark could not go outside to play.
   a. It was raining heavily.
   b. The front door was broken.

2. The ground outside was white.
   a. Someone poured salt over
      the ground.
   b. It snowed during the night.

3. Pam's cat is licking the milk in the bowl.
   a. The cat is hungry.
   b. The cat is cleaning the bowl.

4. Tom took a long nap.
   a. He was tired.
   b. He was looking for something
      to do.

▶**Cause and Effect**

Match the sentences that go together.

Effects	**Causes**
5. Joe's boots are covered with mud.	It began to drizzle.
6. Dad and Jane took an umbrella.	He had a cold.
7. Jill was late for school.	It was nighttime.
8. Tom blew his nose.	He walked in a mud puddle.
9. Bob scored a home run.	She slept too long.
10. Jen turned on the light.	It was hungry.
11. The dog was barking.	He hit the ball over the fence.

COMPREHENSION

▶ # Review

▶ **Past Tense Verbs**

Read each sentence. Circle the past tense verb in each sentence.

1. Grandpa and I drove to the park.

2. Grandpa pushed me on the swings.

3. Then I ran to the jungle gym.

4. I saw my friend Hannah.

5. She smiled at me.

6. We played all day.

UNIT 9 Being Afraid • **Lesson 9** *Something Is There*

▶ **Past Tense Verbs**   ▶ **Review**

Read each sentence. Write the verb that
tells about something that has already
happened.

_____

- - - - - - - - - - - -

7. Amanda and Nick _____ to the party.

        comes   came

_____

- - - - - - - - - - - -

8. The clown _____ balloons.

    bring   brought

_____

- - - - - - - - - - - -

9. The red balloon _____.

       popped   pops

_____

- - - - - - - - - - - -

10. The children _____ games.

      played   plays

_____

- - - - - - - - - - - -

11. Everyone _____ snacks.

    eat   ate

GRAMMAR AND USAGE

Rhythm

Rule	Example
▶ Rhythm is the repeated pattern of a beat.	▶ Frogs go leaping. Frogs leap there. Frogs go leaping Just anywhere!

Read the poems. Draw a line to match the poems that have the same rhythm.

1. Rat-a-tat-tat
   Beats the drum.
   Rat-a-tat-tat
   Taps his thumb!

   Bang, bang, bang
   The hammer goes down.
   Bang, bang, bang
   Build houses in town.

2. Tromp, tromp, tromp
   Twenty marching feet.
   Tromp, tromp, tromp
   Up and down the street.

   Drip-a-drip-drip
   Drops the rain.
   Drip-a-drip-drip
   Down the drain.

▶**Rhythm**

Practice

Read the poem. Use the words in the box to write your own poem using the same rhythm.

Mary had a little lamb,
Little lamb, little lamb,
Mary had a little lamb,
Its fleece was white as snow.

| dog | play | fluffy | day |

_____ _____

Mary had a _____ _____,

_____ _____ _____ _____

_____, _____,

_____ _____

Mary had a _____,

_____ _____

It liked to _____ all _____.

WRITER'S CRAFT

Review

Naming Parts and Action Parts

Read each sentence. Draw a line under the naming part. Circle the verb.

1. Ashley paints flowers.

2. Collin uses yellow paint.

3. Collin and Ashley like art class.

4. They help each other.

UNIT 10 Homes • **Lesson 1** *Unit Introduction*

▶ **Agreement**

▶ **Review**

GRAMMAR AND USAGE

Read each sentence. Write the verb that agrees with the naming part on the line.

_____

5. The baby birds _____ in the nest.

sit   sits

_____

6. Spiders _____ their webs.

spin   spins

_____

7. The bees _____ honey in the hive.

make   makes

_____

8. The frog _____ in the pond.

live   lives

_____

9. The mice _____ in their hole.

hide   hides

_____

10. A cow _____ in the barn.

rest   rests

Classifying

Read the words in the box. Then put
them in the correct group.

brick	leaves	wood	nails
twigs	cement	feathers	sticks

Things people use to
build houses:

_____

1. _____

_____

2. _____

_____

3. _____

_____

4. _____

Things birds use to
build nests:

_____

5. _____

_____

6. _____

_____

7. _____

_____

8. _____

Read the words in the box. Then pick the two words that go together. Write them on the lines.

paper	night	day	pencil
coat	cat	mittens	kitten

_____   _____

9. _____ and _____

10. _____ and _____

11. _____ and _____

12. _____ and _____

Classifying

Put an **X** next to each sentence that tells about animals.

____
1. ____ Baby frogs are called tadpoles.

____
2. ____ The cow grazed on grass in the pasture.

____
3. ____ Mike threw away the sour milk.

____
4. ____ The dog chased the cat around the kitchen.

____
5. ____ The house is made with bricks.

UNIT 10 Homes • **Lesson 4** *A House Is a House for Me*

Read the words in the box. Then put
them in the correct group.

stove	soup	snow	ice cream
fire	ice cubes	oven	freezer

Things that are hot:

_____

6. _____

_____

7. _____

_____

8. _____

_____

9. _____

Things that are cold:

_____

10. _____

_____

11. _____

_____

12. _____

_____

13. _____

COMPREHENSION

Review

Contractions and Apostrophes

Write the contraction on the line. Use an apostrophe to show where letters are missing.

I'm can't they've he's it's

1. he is _____

2. they have _____

3. I am _____

4. it is _____

5. can not _____

UNIT 10 Homes • **Lesson 4** *A House Is a House For Me*

▶ **Contractions and Apostrophes**

 ▶**Review**

Read each contraction. Write the two words that were put together.

6. wasn't _____

_ _ _ _ _ _ _ _ _ _ _ _

_____

8. I'll _____

_ _ _ _ _ _ _ _ _ _ _ _

_____

7. we're _____

_ _ _ _ _ _ _ _ _ _ _ _

_____

9. didn't _____

_ _ _ _ _ _ _ _ _ _ _ _

_____

Read each sentence. Circle the two words that can make a contraction. Write the contraction on the line.

_____

_ _ _ _ _ _ _ _ _ _ _ _

10. I have not seen Meg today.

_____

_____

_ _ _ _ _ _ _ _ _ _ _ _

11. I will walk to Meg's house.

_____

_____

_ _ _ _ _ _ _ _ _ _ _ _

12. Meg is not home.

_____

GRAMMAR AND USAGE

Exact Words

Rule	Example
▶ Use exact words to add details to your writing.	▶ The **tall oak** tree **towers** above other trees. **Crinkly** bark **wraps** around its **sturdy** trunk. Its **long, slender** branches **sway** in the wind.

 **Try It!**

Read the sentences. Draw a line under the exact words.

1. A yellow daffodil bobs gently in the soft breeze.

2. Five round petals surround its bell shaped flower.

3. Honeybees enjoy sipping its sweet nectar.

4. Its ruffled edges curve to the sides.

▶ **Exact Words**

Practice

Draw a picture of your house.

Write exact words to describe it.

Review

▶ Possessive Nouns

Read each sentence. Write the possessive noun in the blank.

1. The bike belongs to Tom.

   _____

   It is _____ bike.

2. The scooter belongs to Amy.

   _____

   It is _____ scooter.

3. That toy belongs to the cat.

   _____

   It is the _____ toy.

4. The dog has a bone.

   _____

   It is the _____ bone.

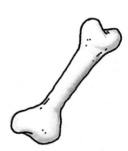

UNIT 10 Homes • **Lesson 5** *Animal Homes*

▶ Possessive Pronouns

▶ Review

Read each sentence.
Write the correct
possessive pronoun in
the blank.

Its	Their	Her	His

5. Randy's dad drives the bus.

    _____

    - - - - - - - - - -

    _____ dad drives the bus.

6. The children's lunches are on the bus.

    _____

    - - - - - - - - - -

    _____ lunches are on the bus.

7. Lori's mom came to help.

    _____

    - - - - - - - - - -

    _____ mom came to help.

8. The elephant's ears are big.

    _____

    - - - - - - - - - -

    _____ ears are big.

Comprehension and Language Arts Skills

GRAMMAR AND USAGE

Main Idea and Details

Read the main idea. Then circle the
sentence that does not belong.
Main Idea: Weather
Details:

1. The snow was melting in the sunshine.

2. It was so cold that the rain turned into
   hail.

3. They went swimming in the pool
   because it was so hot.

4. He had to take a bath because he was
   covered with dirt.

5. The cool air outside made her nose
   cold.

6. His mom drove him to school because
   it was raining.

▶ **Main Idea and Details**

Read the main idea. Then circle the words that do not belong.

Main Idea: Materials used to make shelters
Details:

wood	dirt	grapes
leaves	cement	mud
bricks	nails	cloth
water	sticks	ice
reeds	stones	birds

Sensory Details

Rule	Example
▶ Writers write words that tell how something looks, feels, smells, tastes, and sounds.	▶ Wombats have **white, hairy** noses. They eat **chewy** grass and **soft** roots. Sometimes they make **grunting** sounds.

 **Try It!** Draw a line under the words that tell how something looks, feels, smells, sounds, or tastes.

1. Meerkats make short, sharp, barking sounds.

2. They use their sharp claws to dig.

3. They stay alert in the fresh air.

4. They have round heads and pointed noses.

5. Meerkats eat crunchy beetles.

▶**Sensory Details**

Practice

Write words to finish the sentences.

| white | rocky | short | loud | cool | black | grassy |

6. Zebras have _____ and _____ stripes.

7. They make a _____ whinny sound.

8. Their manes are made of _____ hairs.

9. They drink _____ water out of the river.

10. Some zebras live in _____ hills.

11. Other zebras live on _____ plains.

WRITER'S CRAFT

Making Inferences

Look at the picture. Write three
sentences that explain what might
be happening.

1. _____

   _____

2. _____

   _____

3. _____

▶**Making Inferences**

Read each sentence. Write two possible sentences that explain why each happened.

4. Pat's mother told him to put on his hat and mittens before he went outside. Why?

_____

a. _____

_____

b. _____

5. Sue went into her bedroom and turned on the light. Why?

_____

a. _____

_____

b. _____

COMPREHENSION

▶ Review

▶ Quotation Marks

Read each sentence. Underline the exact words someone says. Circle the name of the speaker.

1. "The farm is a busy place," said Abby.

2. "The hay is in the barn," said Grandpa.

3. "Where are the horses?" asked Rita.

4. "The horses are in the stable," replied Ben.

5. Abby laughed, "The pigs are covered in mud!"

UNIT 10 Homes • **Lesson 7** *Home for a Bunny*

▶ **Quotation Marks**

▶ **Review**

Read the sentences. Write quotation marks at the beginning and end of the exact words someone says.

6. May I feed the cows? asked Rita.

7. Yes, thank you, answered Grandpa.

8. Abby said, The hen laid three eggs.

9. Please gather the eggs in a basket, said Grandpa.

10. Ben rang the bell and yelled, Dinnertime!

11. Grandpa sighed, What a busy day!

MECHANICS

Structure of a Letter

Rule	**Example**
▶ A letter has special parts. The parts of a letter are the date, a greeting, a message, a closing, and your name.	▶ Date: March 14, 2004 Greeting: Dear Shane, Message: We are learning about homes. What are you learning about? Closing: Your friend, Your name: Alex

Try It! Circle the greeting. Draw a line under the date. Draw two lines under the closing. Put a box around the message.

July 6, 2003

Dear Jamie,

  I went to a play. The actors wore animal costumes. They moved just like real animals!

Your friend,

Teri

▶ **Structure of a Letter**

Practice

Write each part of the letter where it belongs.

Your friend,   Dear Chuck,
Samantha   April 27, 2003

_____

- - - - - - - - - - - - - - -

_____   _____

- - - - - - - - - - - - - -

_____

We visited the White House. It is where
the president lives. It is a very large house.
Have you ever been there?

_____

- - - - - - - - - - - - - -

_____

- - - - - - - - - - - - - -

_____

WRITER'S CRAFT

Reality and Fantasy

Circle Reality or Fantasy.

1. Eddie and Sam put up the tent.

   Reality   Fantasy

2. Leo Leopard yelled, "I'm going to jog to the park."

   Reality   Fantasy

3. The pig carefully drove the tractor to the cornfield.

   Reality   Fantasy

4. Rusty walks his dog Dusty every day.

   Reality   Fantasy

5. Wanda Wolf read a bedtime story to her cubs.

   Reality   Fantasy

6. Rachel helped Mom fold the clean clothes.

   Reality   Fantasy

UNIT 10 Homes • **Lesson 9** *The Three Little Pigs*

▶**Reality and Fantasy**

Tell if the sentence is real or a fantasy.
Write **R** or **F** in the box.

7. Dennis picked some strawberries. ☐

8. Hannah melts when she walks in the hot sun. ☐

9. A big gorilla sat and stared at us. ☐

10. The two monkeys danced and sang. ☐

11. The ant carried the picnic basket to the park. ☐

12. Two puppies tugged on the old blanket. ☐

13. Missy the mouse went shopping for new shoes. ☐

14. Chris shouted, "Wait for me!" ☐

COMPREHENSION

▶Review

▶Capital Letters

Read each sentence. Circle each word
that should begin with a capital letter.

1. my friend marta is coming to visit.

2. marta lives in new mexico.

3. i am so excited!

4. marta and i can ride bikes on
beech street.

5. she will be here on monday.

6. spending july with marta will be fun.

UNIT 10 Homes • **Lesson 9** *The Three Little Pigs*

► **Capital Letters**   ►**Review**

Draw a line under the words that should begin with a capital letter. Write the correct capital letter above the word.

7. Uncle greg took us to see fireworks on july fourth.

8. we saw my friends james and chris.

9. i took Marta to jake's pizza for lunch every thursday.

10. It's the best pizza in arizona.

11. Marta left on a sunday.

12. i wrote a letter to marta in september.

Audience and Purpose

Rule	Example
▶ Writers think about the people they are writing for and what they want to tell them.	▶ A music teacher makes a poster to tell the school about a concert. A store owner makes a sign to tell about a sale.

Try It!

Draw a line to match the audience to the purpose.

1. people in a restaurant

2. a gardener

3. a fisherman

4. a cook

a recipe

an ad for a new fishing pole

a menu

directions for growing plants

UNIT 10 Homes • **Lesson 9** *The Three Little Pigs*

► **Audience and Purpose**

WRITER'S CRAFT

Practice

Write the purpose for each audience
on the line.

write a get well card	invite to a party
thank for help	give a report

_____

5. sick friend _____

_____

6. many friends _____

_____

7. a police officer _____

_____

8. your class _____